Fisher-Price

PHONICS

MODERN PUBLISHING
A Division of Unisystems, Inc.
New York, New York 10022
Printed in the U.S.A.
Series UPC #49690

Copyright ©1997, 1999, 2001 by Modern Publishing, a division of Unisystems, Inc.

Fisher-Price and related trademarks, copyrights and character designs are used under license from Fisher-Price, Inc., a subsidiary of Mattel, Inc., East Aurora, NY 14052. U.S.A.
©1997, 1999, 2001 Mattel, Inc. All Rights Reserved. **PRINTED IN THE U.S.A.**
Manufactured for and distributed by Modern Publishing,
a division of Unisystems, Inc., New York, New York 10022.

®Honey Bear Books is a trademark owned by Honey Bear Productions, Inc.,
and is registered in the U.S. Patent and Trademark Office.
No part of this book may be reproduced or copied in any
format without written permission from the publisher.
All Rights Reserved.

Printed in the U.S.A.

NOTE TO PARENTS

Dear Parents:

Helping your children master their world through early learning is as easy as the Fisher-Price® Workbooks!

As your child's first and most important teacher, you can encourage your child's love of learning by participating in learning activities at home. Working together on the activities in each of the Fisher-Price First Grade Workbooks will help your child build confidence, learn to reason, and develop reading, writing, math, and language skills.

Help make your time together enjoyable and rewarding by following these suggestions:

- Choose a quiet time when you and your child are relaxed.
- Provide a selection of writing materials (pens, pencils, or crayons).
- Only work on a few pages at a time. Don't attempt to complete every page if your child becomes tired or loses interest.
- Praise your child's efforts.
- Discuss each page. Help your child relate the concepts in the books to everyday experiences.

Look for these additional Fisher-Price First Grade Workbooks for more early learning fun:

- English
- Reading and Writing
- Math

ESSENTIAL SKILLS

The activities presented in each chapter have been carefully planned, presenting skills at a beginning level and progressing to more challenging activities. Each chapter offers children the opportunity to practice and reinforce basic skills taught in first grade.

Chapter 1   Letters

This chapter encourages children to practice **recognizing upper case and lower case letters**. Children use **auditory discrimination skills** to further their understanding of **beginning, medial, and ending sounds**. As a precursor to dictionary skills, children practice **letter order skills**.

Chapter 2   Vowels

Concepts that help children enhance their **auditory discrimination skills** are used in this chapter. First, children are taught to recognize letters as vowels. Then children are introduced to **long and short vowel sounds**.

Chapter 3   New Sounds

Children learn that **blends are two or three sounds blended together**. They are introduced to more complex sounds and letter combinations such as **r, l, and s blends**. **Consonant digraphs and r-controlled vowels** are presented and practiced in this chapter. Using these phonics skills, children **recognize words** and use their phonics knowledge.

Chapter 4   New Vowel Sounds

Children gain an understanding of **double vowel sounds** and their rules. The vowel spellings **oo, ea, au, aw, ou, ow, oi, oy, and ew** are introduced and practiced by the children. Then children **solve riddles using vowels with irregular patterns**.

Chapter 5   Words

This chapter develops children's **understanding and use of vocabulary**. Children **identify homonyms**. They gain an understanding and learn how to **create compound words**. Children **create new words by adding letters** at the end of a word.

TABLE OF CONTENTS

Letters 6

Vowels 16

New Sounds 25

New Vowel Sounds 41

Words 53

Answer Key 63

LETTERS

Ahoy Mates! Look who's coming into port.
Connect the dots from **a** to **z**.
Then finish coloring the picture.

Skills: Recognizing lower case letters; Practicing letter order

LETTERS

Look at the path to the castle.
There are letters inside each stone.
Write the missing alphabet letters in each empty stone.
Then finish coloring in the picture.

Skills: Understanding letter order

LETTERS

Let's hit some golf balls!
Look at the letter in each golf ball.
Color the golf balls with **lower case** letters one color.
Color the golf balls with **upper case** letters another color.

Skills: Recognizing upper and lower case letters

LETTERS

Look at the pictures on this page.
Look at the letter beside each picture.
Circle the picture if it **begins** with the sound of the letter.
Draw a **line** under the picture if it **ends** with the sound of the letter.

Skills: Developing auditory discrimination; Understanding beginning and ending sounds

LETTERS

It's cool in the shade!
Look at the picture and letter in each pair of glasses.
Color the glasses **green** if the picture **begins** with the sound of the letter.
Color the glasses **brown** if the picture **ends** with the sound of the letter.

Skills: Developing auditory discrimination; Understanding beginning and ending sounds

LETTERS

Watch me make bubbles!
Bubble starts with **b**.
Look at the pictures and letters inside each bubble.
Circle the letter that makes the **beginning sound** of that picture.

Skills: Developing auditory discrimination; Matching beginning sounds

LETTERS

Rack them up!
Pool begins with **p** and ends with **l**.
Look at the pictures and letters inside each pool rack.
Circle the letter that you hear at the **beginning** of each word.
Draw a **line** under the letter that you hear at the **end** of each word.

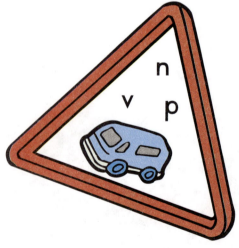

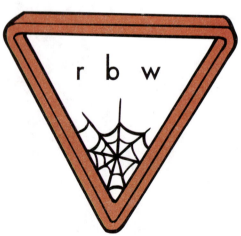

Skills: Developing auditory discrimination; Matching beginning and ending sounds

LETTERS

What's in the middle?
Look at each picture below.
Write the letter for the consonant sound you hear in the **middle** of each word.
The first one is done for you.

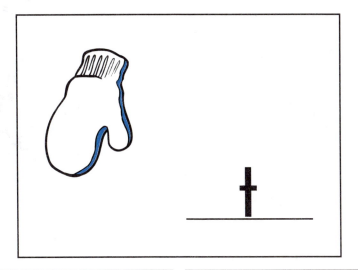

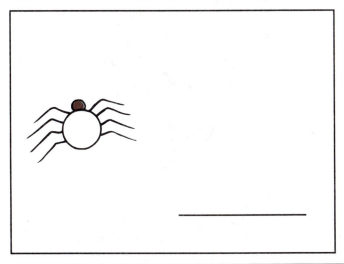

Skills: Developing auditory discrimination; Understanding and recording medial sounds

LETTERS

Can you finish each word?
Look at each picture below.
Write the **middle** letter in the space to complete each word.
Then finish coloring the pictures.

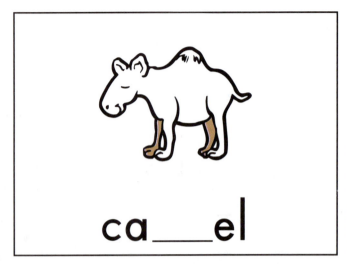
ca___el

ti___er

ru___er

le___on

vio___in

dra___on

Skills: Developing auditory discrimination; Understanding and recording medial sounds

LETTERS

Watch these barrels fly!
Look at the pictures and letters inside each barrel.
Circle the letter you hear in the **middle** of each word.

Skills: Developing auditory discrimination; Understanding and recording medial sounds

VOWELS

The pirates are looking for the real treasure chests.
The real chests have vowels on them.
Look for **A**, **E**, **I**, **O**, **U**.
Color all the chests that have vowels on them.

Skills: Recognizing letters as vowels; Using visual perception skills

VOWELS

Look at this picture.
Find and **circle** the vowels, **a**, **e**, **i**, **o**, **u** hidden in the picture.

Skills: Recognizing letters as vowels; Using visual perception skills

VOWELS

Look at the pictures on the easel.
Track has the **short ă** sound.
Train has the **long ā** sound.
Draw **lines** from the pictures on the easel to the pictures that contain the same vowel sound.

Skills: Using auditory discrimination skills; Differentiating short and long vowel sounds

VOWELS

Look at the pictures on the tree.
Nest has the **short ĕ** sound.
Leaf has the **long ē** sound.
Draw **lines** from the pictures on the tree to the pictures that contain the same vowel sound.

Skills: Using auditory discrimination skills; Differentiating short and long vowel sounds

VOWELS

Look at the pictures on the book.
Mitt has the **short ĭ** sound.
Kite has the **long ī** sound.
Draw **lines** from the pictures on the book to the pictures that contain the same vowel sound.

Skills: Using auditory discrimination skills; Differentiating short and long vowel sounds

VOWELS

Look at the pictures on the mirror.
Sun has the **short ŭ** sound.
Tube has the **long ū** sound.
Draw **lines** from the pictures on the mirror to the pictures that contain the same vowel sound.

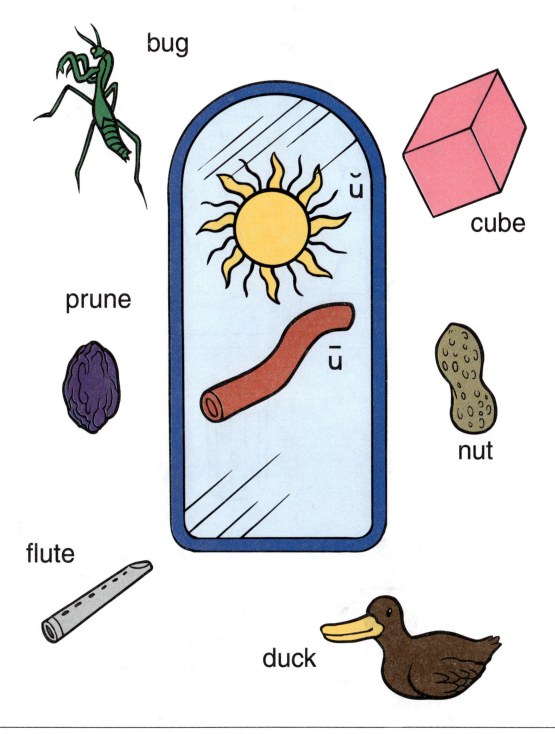

Skills: Using auditory discrimination skills; Differentiating short and long vowel sounds

VOWELS

Look at the pictures in each box. Look at the short vowel letter.
Can you find the picture of a short vowel word to match the letter?
Color the picture that contains the **short vowel** in each box.

Skills: Using auditory discrimination skills; Recognizing short vowel sounds

VOWELS

Look at the pictures in each box. Look at the short vowel letter.
Can you find the picture of a short vowel word to match the letter?
Circle the picture that contains the **short vowel** in each box.

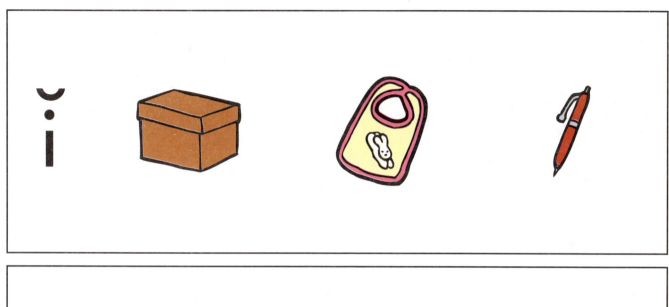

Skills: Using auditory discrimination skills; Recognizing short vowel sounds

VOWELS

Can you find some long vowel words?
Look at the pictures in each balloon.
Color the pictures that contain the same **long vowel sound**.

Skills: Using auditory discrimination skills; Recognizing long vowel sounds

NEW SOUNDS

Train starts with **tr**. **Bridge** starts with **br**.
A blend is two or three consonants sounded together.
Look at the pictures.
Circle the blend that you hear at the **beginning** of each picture.

tr gr fr   br gr cr   dr pr fr

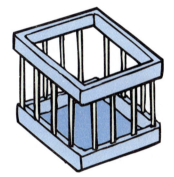

br fr dr   br dr cr   pr fr tr

tr dr cr   dr br fr   gr pr tr

Skills: Identifying r blends; Understanding that blends are two or three sounds blended together

©1997 Fisher-Price, Inc.

NEW SOUNDS

Look at the picture in each truck and say its name.
Draw a **line** to match each picture to the correct word.
Then finish coloring the pictures.

trunk

bread

frame

crown

dress

Skills: Identifying r blends; Recognizing words containing blends; Matching

NEW SOUNDS

Flag starts with **fl**. **Plank** starts with **pl**.
A blend is two or three consonants sounded together.
Look at the pictures.
Circle the blend that you hear at the **beginning** of each picture.

gl cl pl   gl pl fl

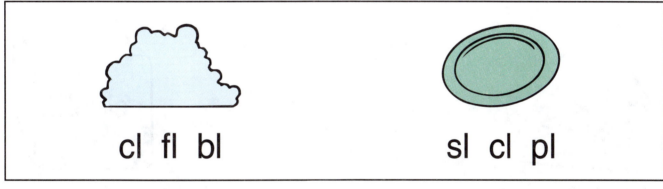

cl fl bl   sl cl pl

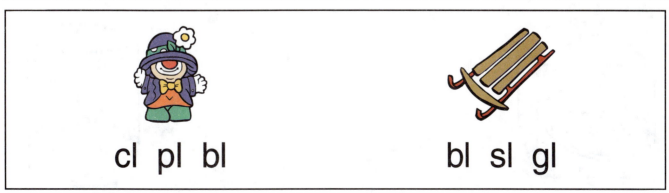

cl pl bl   bl sl gl

Skills: Identifying l blends; Understanding that blends are two or three sounds blended together

NEW SOUNDS

Let's build with these blocks!
Look at the picture in each block on the left.
Look at the word in each block on the right.
Draw a **line** to match each picture to the correct word.

Skills: Identifying l blends; Recognizing words containing blends; Matching

NEW SOUNDS

Swing starts with **sw**. **Slide** starts with **sl**.
A blend is two or three consonants sounded together.
Look at the pictures.
Circle the blend you hear at the **beginning** of each word.

 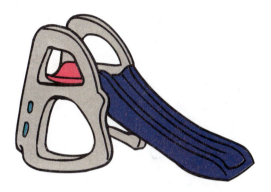

sl sp squ   sc scr sn

sm st scr   sw str sk

sp sc str   squ sl sm

Skills: Identifying s blends; Understanding that blends are two or three sounds blended together

NEW SOUNDS

Look at the pictures in the stars.
Look at the words in the stars.
Draw a **line** to match each picture to the correct word.
Then finish coloring the pictures.

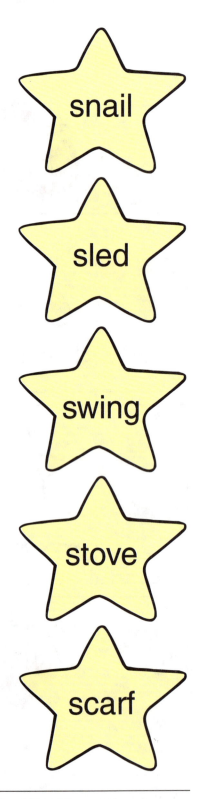

Skills: Identifying s blends; Recognizing words containing blends; Matching

NEW SOUNDS

The word **spy** starts with **sp**. You can play "I Spy."
Look at the pictures on this page.
Read each clue.
Write each answer on the line.

I spy with my little eye something
that shines high in the sky.
I spy a _____.

I spy with my little eye something
that helps you ride on the snow.
I spy a _____.

I spy with my little eye something
that comes out of a chimney.
I spy _____.

I spy with my little eye something
that helps you glide on the ice.
I spy _____.

Skills: Using words containing s blends in context; Recognizing and writing words containing blends

NEW SOUNDS

Chin up! **Thumbs** up!
Look at my new **whistle** and new **shoes**.
Some words have consonant digraphs.
A **digraph** is two letters sounded together to make only one sound.
Look at the picture in each box and say its name.
Circle another picture in each box whose name makes the same sound.

cheese

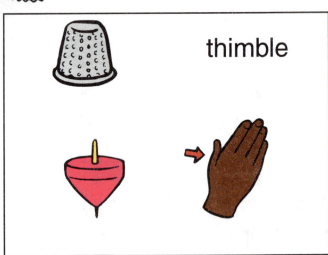
thimble

whale

shirt

Skills: Identifying consonant digraphs; Using auditory discrimination skills

NEW SOUNDS

The word **block** ends with the consonant digraph **-ck**.
A **digraph** is two letters sounded together to make only one sound.
Look at the pictures below.
Say the name of each picture.
Then **circle** the letters that stand for the consonant digraph you hear at the end of each word.

ch   sh   th

th   sh   ck

ck   sh   ch

ck   th   ch

sh   th   ch

sh   ck   th

Skills: Identifying consonant digraphs at the end of words; Using auditory discrimination skills

NEW SOUNDS

Say the word **car**.
The **-r** after the **a** changes the vowel sound.
Look at the pictures on this page.
Color the ones that have a vowel sound with **-r** like car.

Skills: Understanding r-controlled vowels; Using auditory discrimination

NEW SOUNDS

Say the word **store**.
The **-r** after the **o** changes the vowel sound.
Look at the things in the store.
Circle the ones that have a vowel sound with **-r** like store.

Skills: Understanding r-controlled vowels; Using auditory discrimination

NEW SOUNDS

Look at the picture and the word **girl**.
The **-r** after the **i** changes the vowel sound.
Trace the word girl.
Then say the name of each picture below.
Read the words beside each picture.
Circle the word that names each picture.

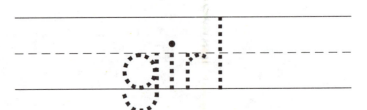

barn
bun
bird

skip
scarf
skirt

short
shirt
ship

Skills: Understanding r-controlled vowels; Recognizing words

NEW SOUNDS

Look at the picture and the word **fern**.
The **-r** after the **e** changes the vowel sound.
Trace the word fern.
Look at the words in the box. Look at the pictures below.
Write the correct word to match each picture.

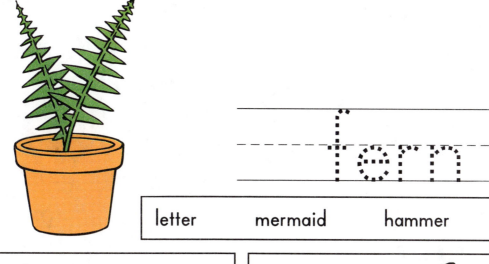

| letter | mermaid | hammer | spider |

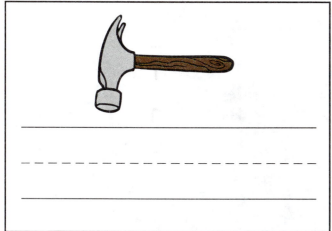

Skills: Understanding r-controlled vowels; Recognizing and writing words

NEW SOUNDS

Say the word **turkey**.
The **-r** after the **u** changes the vowel sound.
Look at the pictures on this page.
Color the ones that have a vowel sound with **-r** like turkey.

Skills: Understanding r-controlled vowels; Using auditory discrimination

NEW SOUNDS

Play a game using the letter pairs **ar**, **er**, **ir**, **or**, and **ur**.
Read each sentence below.
Follow the directions of each sentence.
Then color the rest of the page.

Draw a face on the star. Then circle the letters ar.

Give the horse a bucket of oats. Then draw a line under the letters or.

Draw more leaves on the fern. Then draw a box around the letters er.

Make a nest for the bird. Then put dots above the letters ir.

Draw a hat on the nurse. Then put dots under the letters ur.

Skills: Practicing r-controlled vowels; Following 2-step directions

NEW SOUNDS

Think about the sounds these letter pairs make — **ar**, **er**, **ir**, **or**, and **ur**.
Look at the pictures and letters below.
Circle the letter pair that you hear in the name of each picture.

ar   ur   ir

or   ir   ar

ur   er   or

ur   ar   ir

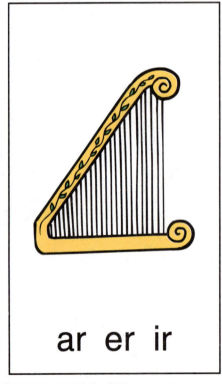

ar   er   ir

ar   or   er

Skills: Practicing r-controlled vowels; Identifying sounds in words

NEW VOWEL SOUNDS

Let's feed the animals **hay** and **grain**.
The **ay** and **ai** in each word make the long $\bar{a}$ sound.

Draw lines to match each word on the left with a picture on the right.

pail

tray

train

chain

Skills: Understanding double vowels and their rules; Identifying sounds in words; Matching

NEW VOWEL SOUNDS

The **queen** invited everyone to a **feast**.
The **ee** and **ea** in each word make the long ē sound.

Look at the scene below.
Look at the words in the box.
Put an **X** on the picture that shows each word from the box.

| queen   beach   beak   tree   leash   peas   sheep |

Skills: Understanding double vowels and their rules; Matching words to pictures

NEW VOWEL SOUNDS

Joe has a slice of **pie**.
The **oe** and **ie** in each word make a long vowel sound.

Look at the pictures below.
Look at the words in the box.
Write the word that matches each picture on the line under each picture.

| tie | flies | hoe | toe | fries |

_____   _____

   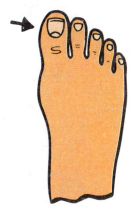

_____   _____

Skills: Understanding double vowels and their rules; Matching words to pictures

NEW VOWEL SOUNDS

José likes to **row** his **boat**.
The **ow** and **oa** in each word make a long vowel sound.

Look at the pictures below.
Find and circle the words in the puzzle grid.

```
d e f c r w w t l u m l p
b i v d s c u l b o w g m
o s o a p o k o i x n s p
a n o i w a b m y l n o s
t i o w e t u w o a s v c
```

boat

bow

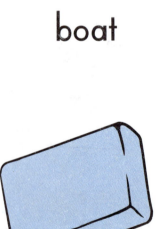

soap

coat

Skills: Understanding vowel sounds; Visual perception; Matching words to pictures

NEW VOWEL SOUNDS

Put your **foot** in the **boot**.
Sometimes a double vowel makes a new sound.
Think about the sounds that **oo** makes in foot and boot.

Look at the pictures and words.
Say the name of each picture.
If the vowel sound is like the **oo** in boot, write the word in the **boot**.
If the vowel sound is like **oo** in foot, write the word in the **foot**.

book   moon   hook   spoon   hood   moose   broom

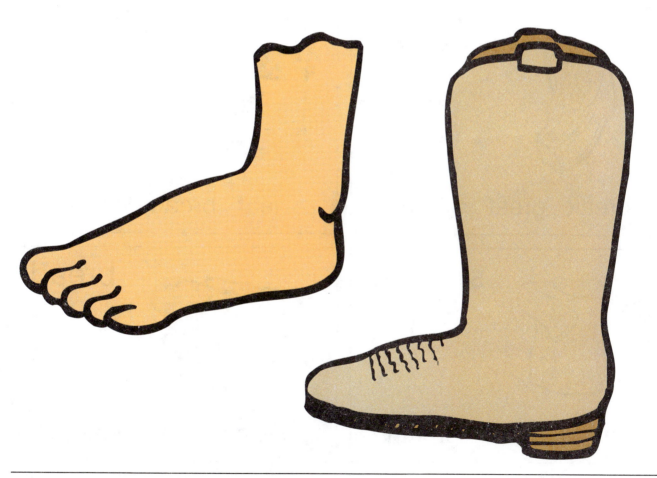

Skills: Recognizing the irregular sounds of oo; Writing

NEW VOWEL SOUNDS

This is **great bread**!
Sometimes a double vowel makes a new sound.
Think about the sounds that **ea** makes in great and bread.

Look at the pictures and words in each box.
Say the name of each picture.
If a word in the list makes the same **ea** sound as the pictured word, put a **circle** around it. There may be more than one answer.

feather	break

bread head peas	great beak steak

steak	thread

break great dream	leaf bread head

sweater	bread

leather bead breath	ready seal heavy

Skills: Recognizing the irregular sounds of ea

NEW VOWEL SOUNDS

Can you **draw** a **haunted** house?
Sometimes a double vowel makes a new sound.
Think about the sound that **aw** makes in draw
and **au** makes in haunted.

Look at the words in the box.
Read each sentence below.
Find the correct word to complete each sentence.

| paws | caught | claws | saucer |

My cat is white and has four black _____.

Her _____ are a little sharp.

I put milk in a _____ for my cat.

My cat _____ a mouse yesterday.

Skills: Recognizing the irregular sounds of au and aw; Completing sentences; Writing

NEW VOWEL SOUNDS

Say the name of the picture in each cannon.
Circle the pictures in each row of cannon balls whose names have the same vowel sound.
Then finish coloring the page.

Skills: Recognizing words that have the same vowel sound

NEW VOWEL SOUNDS

We planted **flowers** in the **ground**.
Sometimes a double vowel makes a new sound.
Think about the sound that **ow** makes in flowers and **ou** makes in ground.

Look at the words in the flowers.
Look at the words on the ground.
Then read each riddle and write the answer on the line.

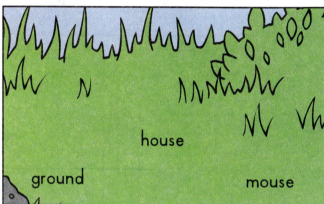

The prince wears it on his head. _____

This is a place a person might live. _____

These grow in the ground and are very pretty. _____

This is the dirt in which plants grow. _____

You dry yourself with this cloth. _____

This is a little animal with a long tail. _____

Skills: Recognizing the vowel sounds of ou and ow; Writing

NEW VOWEL SOUNDS

The **boy** has a collection of **coins**.
Sometimes a double vowel makes a new sound.
Think about the sound that **oy** makes in boy and **oi** makes in coins.

Look at each picture and say its name.
Find the word in the box that matches each picture and write it on the line.

Skills: Recognizing the vowel sounds of oi and oy; Writing

NEW VOWEL SOUNDS

We **threw** my **new** ball.
Think about the sound that **ew** makes in threw and new.

Look at the words in the box.
Complete each sentence by finding the missing word in the box.

| drew | grew | few | new | blew |

I have a _____ box of crayons.

Pretty flowers _____ in the garden.

A _____ birds sat on the fence.

The wind _____ the leaves off the trees.

Do you like the picture I _____ ?

Skills: Recognizing the vowel sounds of ew; Writing

NEW VOWEL SOUNDS

Read each riddle below.
Write the word from the box that completes each riddle.

| boy | dime | cow | house | clown | stew |

I wear funny clothes.
I have a red nose.
Who am I? _____

You can live in me.
I have windows and a door.
What am I? _____

I am cooked on a stove.
I have vegetables and meat.
What am I? _____

I am not a girl.
I will grow up to be a man.
Who am I? _____

I give you milk.
I have four legs and a tail.
What am I? _____

I am round and metal.
I am used as money.
What am I? _____

Skills: Solving riddles using vowels that have irregular patterns; Writing

WORDS

Words that sound the same but are spelled differently and have different meanings are called **homonyms**.

Sew and **so** are homonyms.

Look at the picture and words in each box. Draw a **circle** around the word that has the same meaning as the picture.

   cent   sent

   son   sun

   to   two

   tale   tail

Skills: Identifying homonyms; Visual perception; Matching words to pictures

WORDS

Words that sound the same but are spelled differently and have different meanings are called **homonyms**.

Tow and **toe** are homonyms.

Look at the picture and words in each box. Draw a **circle** around the word that has the same meaning as the picture.

 pail   pale

 see   sea

 dear   deer

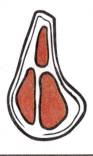 meat   meet

Skills: Identifying homonyms

WORDS

Words that sound the same but are spelled differently and have different meanings are called **homonyms**.

Blue and **blew** are homonyms.

Look at the word on each hamburger.
Look at the word on each bun.
Draw a **line** to match the words that are homonyms.

Skills: Identifying homonyms; Matching

WORDS

Words that sound the same but are spelled differently and have different meanings are called **homonyms**.

Beet and **beat** are homonyms.

Look at the pairs of homonyms in the box.
Read the sentences.
Complete each sentence using a word from the box.

| sent | cent | son | sun | sail | sale |

The _____ is shining in the sky.

A penny is another name for a _____ .

Put the _____ up on the ship.

I _____ a letter to you.

This is my _____ and daughter.

The hats in the store are for _____ .

Skills: Using homonyms to complete a sentence; Writing

WORDS

Make a **compound** word by putting two words together!

Look at each picture and the word below it.
Put each pair of words together to make a new word.
Write the compound word on the line.

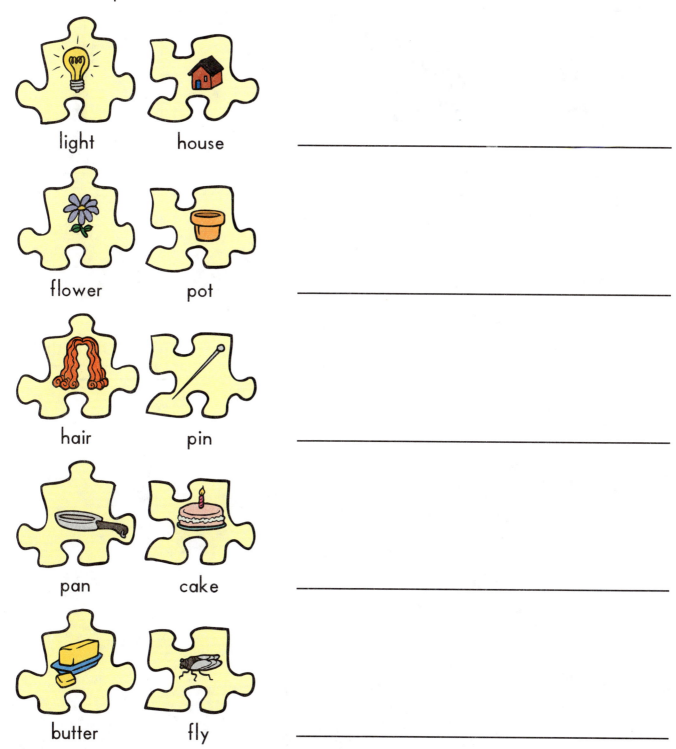

Skills: Understanding and creating compound words; Writing

WORDS

Draw a **line** between the two words that make each **compound** word to make two smaller words.
Then write and draw a picture of your own compound word.

horsefly

wheelchair

lighthouse

mailbox

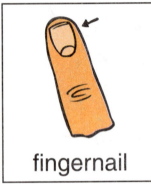
fingernail

birdbath

teapot

football

Skills: Identifying individual parts of compound words; Writing and drawing

WORDS

Make a **compound** word by putting two words together!
Look at the words in the box.
Find each word in the puzzle below.
Then make compound words using these words.

| wheel   work   sun   tea   sea   chair   bench   flower   spoon   shell |

_____

_____

_____

_____

_____

Skills: Understanding and creating compound words; Writing

WORDS

Watch this magic trick!
If you add an **e** to the end of some words, the sound of the vowel changes and becomes a long vowel sound.
Can + e becomes **cane**.

Look at the words and pictures below.
Write the new word and draw a **line** to the picture that shows what the new word says.

man + e _____

cape

kit + e _____

mane

pin + e _____

kite

cap + e _____

pane

pan + e _____

pine

Skills: Understanding how words can change; Creating new words; Writing

WORDS

If you add an **e** to the end of some words, the sound of the vowel changes and becomes a long vowel sound.
Tub + e become **tube**.

Look at the pictures below.
Each picture has two words under it.
Circle the word that names the picture.
Color the pictures if the magic **e** made the vowel a long vowel.

tap   tape

van   vane

plane   plan

spin   spine

dim   dime

fin   fine

Skills: Understanding how words can change

WORDS

If you add an **e** to the end of some words, the sound of the vowel changes and becomes a long vowel sound.
Van + **e** becomes **vane**.

Read each sentence below.
Look at the two words beside each sentence.
Draw a **line** under the word that completes the sentence and write it on the line.
Put an **X** next to the word that has a long vowel sound.

We _____ paintings in art class.   mad   made

Wipe your feet on the _____ .   mat   mate

I have a nickel and a _____ .   dim   dime

Who will _____ the game?   win   wine

I _____ my bicycle to school.   rid   ride

Take your _____ and gloves.   hat   hate

Skills: Understanding how words can change; Writing

ANSWER KEY

Page 6

Page 7
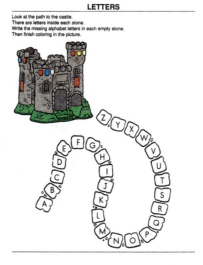

Page 8
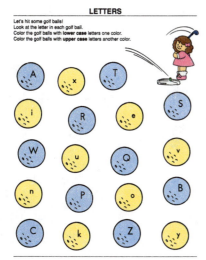

Page 9

Page 10

Page 11

ANSWER KEY

Page 12

Page 13

Page 14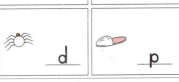

Page 15

Page 16

Page 17

©1997 Fisher-Price, Inc.

ANSWER KEY

Page 18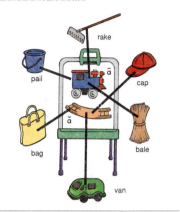

Page 19

Page 20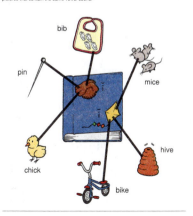

Page 21

Page 22

Page 23

©1997 Fisher-Price, Inc.

ANSWER KEY

Page 24
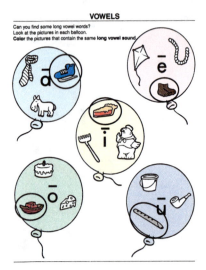

Page 25

Page 26
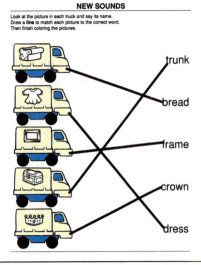

Page 27
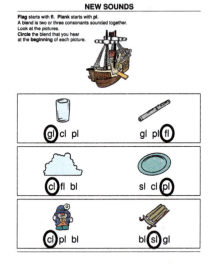

Page 28
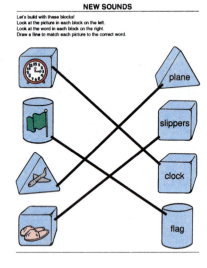

Page 29
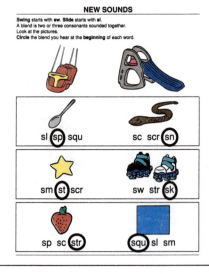

66 ©1997 Fisher-Price, Inc.

ANSWER KEY

Page 30

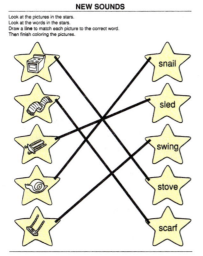

Page 31

Page 32

Page 33

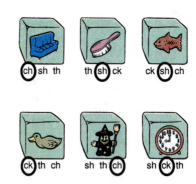

Page 34

Page 35

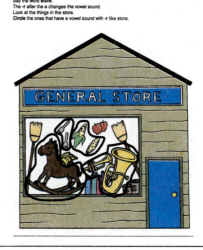

ANSWER KEY

Page 36

Page 37

Page 38

Page 39

Page 40

Page 41

©1997 Fisher-Price, Inc.

ANSWER KEY

Page 42

Page 43

Page 44

Page 45

Page 46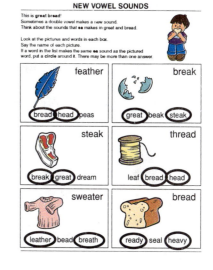

Page 47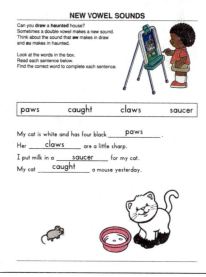

©1997 Fisher-Price, Inc.

ANSWER KEY

Page 48

NEW VOWEL SOUNDS
Say the name of the picture in each cannon.
Circle the pictures in each row of cannon balls whose names have the same vowel sound.
Then finish coloring the page.

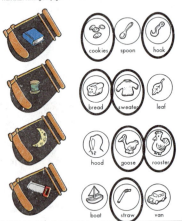

Row 1: cookies, spoon, hook
Row 2: bread, sweater, leaf
Row 3: hood, goose, rooster
Row 4: boat, straw, van

Page 49

NEW VOWEL SOUNDS
We planted **flowers** in the **ground**.
Sometimes a double vowel makes a new sound.
Think about the sound that **ow** makes in flowers and **ou** makes in ground.

Look at the words in the flowers.
Look at the words on the ground.
Then read each riddle and write the answer on the line.

Flowers: crown, towel, flowers
Ground: house, ground, mouse

The prince wears it on his head. — crown
This is a place a person might live. — house
These grow in the ground and are very pretty. — flowers
This is the dirt in which plants grow. — ground
You dry yourself with this cloth. — towel
This is a little animal with a long tail. — mouse

Page 50

NEW VOWEL SOUNDS
The **boy** has a collection of **coins**.
Sometimes a double vowel makes a new sound.
Think about the sound that **oy** makes in boy and **oi** makes in coins.

Look at each picture and say its name.
Find the word in the box that matches each picture and write it on the lines.

boy   coins   toys   oil   soil   point

coins | oil | toys
point | boy | soil

Page 51

NEW VOWEL SOUNDS
We **threw** my **new** ball.
Sometimes a double vowel makes a new sound.
Think about the sound that **ew** makes in threw and new.

Look at the words in the box.
Complete each sentence by finding the missing word in the box.

drew   grew   few   new   blew

I have a __new__ box of crayons.
Pretty flowers __grew__ in the garden.
A __few__ birds sat on the fence.
The wind __blew__ the leaves off the trees.
Do you like the picture I __drew__?

Page 52

NEW VOWEL SOUNDS
Read each riddle below.
Write the word from the box that completes each riddle.

boy   dime   cow   house   clown   stew

I wear funny clothes.
I have a red nose.
Who am I? — clown

You can live in me.
I have windows and a door.
What am I? — house

I am cooked on a stove.
I have vegetables and meat.
What am I? — stew

I am not a girl.
I will grow up to be a man.
Who am I? — boy

I give you milk.
I have four legs and a tail.
What am I? — cow

I am round and metal.
I am used as money.
What am I? — dime

Page 53

WORDS
Words that sound the same but are spelled differently and have different meanings are called **homonyms**.

Sew and **so** are homonyms.

Look at the picture and words in each box.
Draw a circle around the word that has the same meaning as the picture.

(cent)   sent
son   (sun)
to   (two)
tale   (tail)

©1997 Fisher-Price, Inc.

ANSWER KEY

Page 54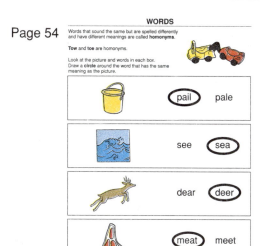

Page 55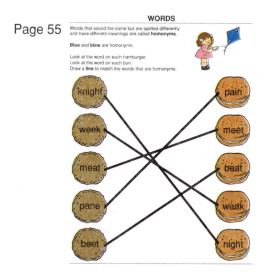

Page 56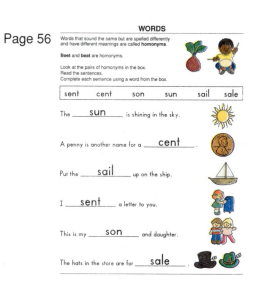

Page 57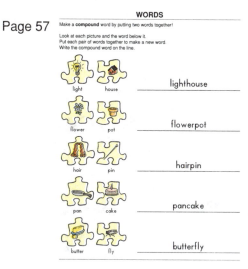

Page 58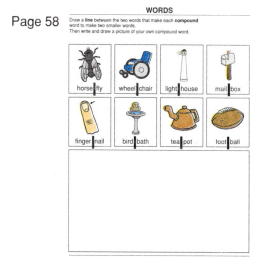

Page 59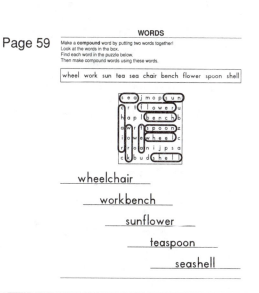

ANSWER KEY

Page 60

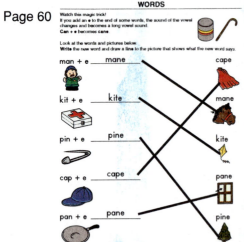

Page 61

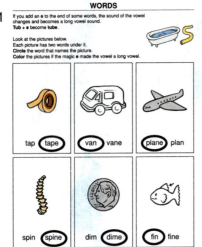

Page 62

We __made__ paintings in art class.   mad   __made__ X

Wipe your feet on the __mat__.   __mat__   mate X

I have a nickel and a __dime__.   dim   __dime__ X

Who will __win__ the game?   __win__   wine X

I __ride__ my bicycle to school.   rid   __ride__ X

Take your __hat__ and gloves.   __hat__   hate X